The Bear's Mouth

Other Books by Laura Stott:

Blue Nude Migration

In the Museum of Coming and Going

THE BEAR'S MOUTH

Laura Stott

LynxHousePress
SPOKANE, WASHINGTON

FIRST EDITION

Lynx House Press
lynxhousepress.com

Cover Design: Jodi Miller-Hunter
Interior Design: Aimee R. Thompson

Cover Art: Katheryn Stott Buxton

Author Photo: Jake Rogers

Cataloging-in-publication data may be obtained from the Library of
Congress.

ISBN 978-0-89924-199-9

For Jane, Tori, and Emma

Contents

Think of the wren
and how little flesh is needed to make a song.

-Galway Kinnell

Safe Keeping

A songbird's nest nestled inside a glass jar,
a clear vessel made of sand collected from a shore
so far from here we can't comprehend the ocean,
what desert, what mountain
bumped up against an ancient lake
millions of years gone. I collect fossils
of fish, palms, birds entombed in mud, then rock.
What killed them together there?
Only to be broken open
by my hands with some tools for splitting
shale. Layer by layer, like sheets of heavy paper.
A tourist on holiday. The guide shows us
how to do it. Each layer lifted
reveals a fin—something ancient
that was hunted swims.
The waves, older than any of us,
carried this sand, perhaps even
a prehistoric beach,
collected and melted to glass,
to form a clear place—
a vessel turned orbuculum.
And if you look inside,
you'll see a mother and a child
on a hike one winter in a slim canyon.
After they lost a daughter, a sister.
They plucked an abandoned nest
from a red dogwood's spindly arms
and carried it home. Waxwing. Warbler.
Gravity carries it all
towards the center of the earth,
and the tide, towards some other center—
something in the sky, without a sea,
but numerous shores.

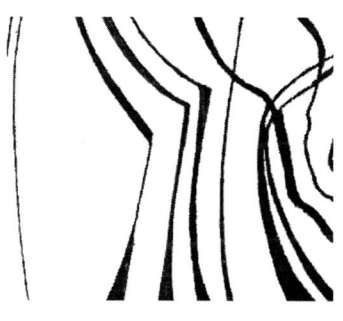

I

Reaching Inside

In the book of myths, a little girl with brown hair, pigtails, runs through the woods, trailing a line of flowers behind her—columbine, buttercup, harebell, monk's hood.

You have to be your own Cerberus, the book says.

To enter this story, you have to climb through a window and out that window, there are countless lives. An ocean with tall angry waves, a tent on the shore, a helicopter disappears between clouds and mountain peaks. A glacier cracks, splits open and we all fall inside. A green river rises full of silt and rock and blood. But there is no three-headed dog, only one pup sleeping in the sunshine. A pool of drool. There goes the girl, with her bouquet of sunlight, she's almost to the clearing where the meadow begins, and a cabin sits at the edge of a lake where her mother and father sit in the sun and weep. Full of grief. There, the girl waves.

There is no witch coming. There is no ogre at the end of the dark tunnel.

Just her mom and dad, weeping. But they still can't believe how beautiful it all is. Like this is heaven, here on the edge of the lake. And there also, a younger and an older sister, waving to her from shore.

In this story, the girl runs into the meadow with her flowers where she sees the bear, the one large enough for her to crawl inside. She walks up to its afternoon laziness while it digs in the ground, and the bear stops and lifts her massive head and sniffs the air. She's guarding the underworld. The girl drops the flowers and the bear looks right at the girl. In the story—I've climbed in now too, through the same window, *past my own monster*—I'm following the trail of flowers until I see the light, the break in the trees, and I climb over the rocks. The pack I'm carrying is heavy and the trail steep. There is the meadow. I look and I look. I see myself on the shore in the distance, crying, sunlight on my face. And there

there is the bear. I walk up and I say to the bear, *Do you have her?* The bear opens her great mouth and I stick my head inside. Her teeth graze my skull. I look hard and I listen, until I hear the great heart beating again.

She Is Hungry

Winter opens its cold hand.

In the palm

is a smooth, black stone,
the pupil

in the bear's eye.

Spring has come.

Tracking the Bear

The bear crosses the river and makes her rounds from bush to tree to mud. Digs at grubs. These claws can tear both flesh and earth, rip boulders out of her way. The muscle she carries on her bones can make her seven-hundred pounds run 35 miles an hour, low to the ground, not sleekness but power. Yet right now she lies lazy in the sun, dreaming the creation of fish and devil's club. In a moment, she'll rise again. From a distance, she's all teddy bear. Something you may want to hug. Above her in the air, a swoop, a sedge, a siege of cranes moves north. That primal sound that means *forever*. Look up. Waiting there.

The only way to hold the hand of who's lost is to get past this bear. But I can see each claw, four inches long.

In a moment she'll yawn, rise and move her heft of weight any way she wants to across tidal flats to a dark space in the woods, where the trees grow moss on their backs and arms, where the lichen oozes pink, where the damp is everywhere and the bear can disappear into a forest where it smells like the beginning
of everything.

Feast

The bear eats the brains of the fish.
Plucks them out of the water with bear mouth
and claw, one fish, one brain after another.
Practicing economy. Skin, eggs, heads.
The fat and flesh of minds. She leaves body
after body on the bank. When a baby
is the size of a blueberry,
it's growing 100 brain cells a minute.
A constellation, a map of stories
that will contain the memory of animals,
of moss, of father's cool, rough hand
in the heat of a fever. *There there, little one—*
in the sky of your mind
the story of the tiger
still exists. They are on earth yet
and hide in the jungle, imagine it.
Hope for one hundred more.
In Alaska, the blueberries fill bottles, bowls.
Every secret blueberry spot kept safe—*across the lake,*
this side of the bridge, up West Creek, don't tell.
Pieces of tart night sky.
Bears eat them by the fistful.
Blueberries glistening in fresh scat.
The salmon have returned
after years of the deep, a fjord
echoing with the sound of ice
long carving the mountains gone.
What shore receded from here?
The bodies of fish scatter the river bank
and the eagles wait, spread their wingspan wide
before they land, like a dragon
scavenging the earth.

Ink

The tattoo I don't have is of a million birds hidden on my body, a million birds with dark wings or bright wings, traveling across vast oceans, to a nesting place. They are somewhere no one can see them on my body. They are singing: sudden in the sunlight, the chickadee perched sideways on the porch railing. The smallest hummingbird investigating the mouth of a flower. The terns that fly from one hemisphere to another, their sharp, bone butterfly wings darting over the fjord. The cranes, there, painted on the skin of air, flying above your head, a primal sound in their throats. A million years. The raven in Alaska that hops behind cars in the rain and disappears into the mist of a strip mall parking lot, just disappears, while a woman and a child chase it. The blue heron that holds still in the water, great and still, waiting for a small silver fish to swim into its shade and rest in the cool of its captor's body that is somewhere in the pond of my body. Only to be swallowed whole. As fast as you can blink.

Dance

2 ½ years after the fact, a certificate of stillbirth from the state arrives in the mail.

After 75 mile per hour winds, we lose power. Day five as night falls, a cricket sings in the bathroom.

On a hike we spot a long-eared owl trying to sleep in the morning sun. He looked just like the fallen tree he dozed on.

In their migration, butterflies try to fly over the mountain. The wind sends them back over and over.

No rain this summer
and when it finally comes in September, we find a dead garter snake on the doormat.

My daughter and I put the snake in a baby rice cracker box with moss and leaves for a pillow.

In quarantine, we all put silly dresses on and dance in the living room.

We put the cricket in a jar to carry it outside. And just then the lights come back on.

Fritillary or painted lady.

Two racoons crawl up the side of the chicken pen. Stare the critters in the eye. Small bears?

My toddler won't stop trying to climb anything she can find.

Another snake slips away under the bird bath and into the basil.

A small family of finches chirp, each one a symbol for resurrection.

It's always been a dream of my mom's to see the Aurora Borealis.

I love watching my oldest run.
It is pure joy on her face. Like it's the best thing in the world to feel her body move fast
and to be out of breath.
I wonder what finish lines I'll watch her cross.

The health department told me they didn't have a record of my baby.
I'm sorry.

8 thousand dollars say I spent 22 hours in Labor and Delivery.

The bees are drinking juice from the concord grapes now.
Grape vines so heavy, they are tearing down the fence. Each one looks like a planet.

We chase the racoons away in our bare feet.
Close the coop door.

2 years later, I find the paper with a sticker and a barcode and the name we gave her, and send it in.

Five eggs a day.
Imperfect moons my daughter gathers and carries inside.

Mushrooms grow on a tree like flowers from outer space.

Once, even a few times, before any of this,
I watched the northern lights dance. Ethereal body of green.

September strawberries my baby stuffs in her mouth, her hand flat and like a star
over her lips once the fruit makes it in.

A strange life moving across the sky.

Predation

Instinct tells us to howl
or sing, to find someone to love.
Here, take this fish, fresh
from the cool lake, life gone
after the frantic twist
of body in the grass, on the rocks, *Oh,*
hold still fish.
The hook, no barb, slides easy
out of the white mouth,
row of trout teeth, a skyline
before throat.

If I keep this one, I'll slap
its head against a rock.

I watched my dad as a child
kill fish this way—*Wham!*
One is all it took.
But it takes me many more.

Which is why I hate it.
The moon in the eye of the fish
disappears so suddenly, why
does that surprise me? The light gone.
The eye in the sky
is pulling all of us
towards something else.
Whole oceans at a time disappear.
The moon and a sound
in the lung.

Monster

Spider webs by the back door funnel into
a black cave, a silk and nocturnal universe
where a fanged creature waits
for the moon's threaded children—
a moth, a mantisfly—
to step gently into the tangle
of reflection.

Mother spider wraps her legs lovingly
around all her young and whispers,
This is the earth
you are waiting to be born into—
dream of the wings you'll eat,
and kingdoms between roses.

What Are These Hearts That Sleep

all winter under earth's skin?
Tulip bulbs. Spears cutting
out of the black,
arms to the sky, bright mouths
opening in song.
This ritual. Rebirth after rebirth.
Call it resurrection.
From another world, secrets sweet
telling on their tongues.

Sisters

My daughter cries, *Hello, deer*
when we drive down the highway in the dark,
past the woods, when we hike the trail,
when she eats her breakfast and holds her spoon in the air.
          And there they are, the deer in my kitchen,
ears twitching, wide eyes staring at the toddler while she smiles,
so pleased at calling them here.
But what now?
Hello, baby, she says, and puts her head against my belly
where a tiny hand waves from a nearby shore.
The lake ripples with rain. The trees hush/grow quiet.
I hope she hears you, little one.
The doctors say the baby's survival is impossible.
Your hands won't ever get to touch.
When to tell her?
Somewhere in the dark, she sees what we don't, in my tunnel,
off the road, the deer's eyes peer back at her, glinting silver in the dark,
their bodies perched and ready to jump.
                              I reach down
to pick something that shines off the kitchen floor.
Hello baby, hello deer.

Opening

I walk this cemetery
where your tiny body must have raised up
from the incinerator as smoke.
Your hands, the size of coins,
disappeared faster than any of us can imagine.
I'd like to imagine them turning into hands perfectly
a second time, uncurling in the light.
Starlings hide in the trees
shouting. The sound I catch
but I can't see the hundreds of wings
folded there. Loud
and hopeful things.
This morning, I opened
the door of my home,
before the murmur,
before the dust cloud of bone
and ink
rose in the shape
of animal—a black whale
in the sky
that sings.

Can You Hear Me?

You've turned into a whale. Like magic, there you are, under the surface, swimming past me. I look over the edge of a dock into the deep and watch your body down there, chase it as far as I can. How far am I willing to go? From one ship dock to another. Something this large. Something that sings. I once sang to you in my body. There you are. You dive jubilant into the blue, the glacial green.

Beneath

Who breathes out a sigh like the largest living animal on earth?
I say she is a whale gliding through the fjord, a canyon
holding the depth of an ocean
because I don't know how else she might have looked.

She is a whale gliding through the fjord, a canyon.
She is my daughter, a brown-haired wonder,
because I don't know how else she might have looked,
a creature below the surface of everything.

She is my daughter, like her sisters, another brown-haired wonder.
I remember sitting on a rocky shore in a past life, evening,
while a creature swam below the surface of everything.
I watched a light blinking across the fjord, the other side

of a rocky shore in a past life. Even then
I could hear the whale sing, the sound of her coming up for air
across the fjord—like a light signaling on the other side.
A forever wonder, the sound of that voice.

I could hear a whale sing, but not the sound of my baby coming up for air.
Here is a blanket that once held her body.
I will forever wonder what her voice would have sounded like.
I pull a box down from the shelf that holds everything—

a blanket that once held her body.
The texture of it on my fingertips is all I have left.
I pull a box down from the shelf that holds everything.
A container for her after she died inside me.

The texture of my own fingertips is all I have left.
Suddenly a blue jay wakes the world as
a container for, after she died inside me.
Sometimes I want to believe it's her on the trail I'm hiking—

a sudden blue jay that wakes the world, like

the whales that surface to let us know they are there.
Sometimes I want to believe it is her on the trail hiking—
I'm here I'm here, how beautiful it all is,

like the whales that surface to let us know they are there.
All the moments I wish I could go back and live again:
I'm here I'm here. How beautiful, her sisters' laughter.
My baby's fingers were pressed together like a Buddha.

All the moments I wish I could go back and live again.
I would ask the nurse to monitor the heartbeat until its last.
My baby's fingers were pressed together like a Buddha
who breathes out a sigh like the largest living animal on earth.

4am

like the tide comes in. It slowly floods
the house like a cold wave
bringing in seaweed, old sneakers, octopus arms
disguised. Fish to hide in the white shells
of your mind. A beached whale
fills the entire house with its suffering.

In Sleep, Baby Jane

At the 3am feeding, I swear, I can hear the milk
from my body hitting your stomach,
it's entering like rain into rain.
The water of your body swallowing
the echo of the moon in this dark room.
Outside, it's so cold this December
that everything breaks
under any kind of weight.
The trees are covered in a fine sheen
of looking glass. I move the curtain back
to see if the aquarium holds any life yet.
There's only a pane of glass
between us and this ocean.
Heaven. The road is white and quiet.
where an owl glides between worlds,
pulled by an invisible string.
She carries a stone in her talon.
Everyone will one day learn how to swim.
The highway is closed tonight for ice
because out there, too many slid off the road
and a family mourns.
There was a moment just before
the world began to spin.
And the owl drops the stone
where a fish, out of the dark,
swallows it whole.
Here, in this room, my tiny angel eats
with her eyes closed,
hands clenched in the smallest fists,
swaddled still, close
to the heat of my body.
We're both still in a dream.
When I pick you up out of your cry,
your lips purse into a kiss.
Coming up for air. Growing larger
as we breathe, under the ceiling
and tide of the room.

Talking to the Bear

-For Dylan

After the bear grabs his leg with its mouth
shakes him around, drags him a bit, finally lets go,
starts to circle him on the ground,
my friend talks to the bear, even as the bear's teeth
break his leg, *hey, it's cool, Bear. Be cool.*
After the circles get wider,
he reaches to his backpack, still on his back,
going for the bear spray, and the bear charges him again,
stops short and face to face,
opens her mouth wide and roars.
Point made. *Okay, okay.*
I understand. The bear circles him again.
She doesn't eat him.
She just wants him to know who is in charge.
Late October. No one else is on the trail, he's 7 miles in.
The paw print later measures at 7 inches across. Just a juvenile.
He makes a splint, irrigates the wound, the place where the teeth sank in,
and makes his way to a cabin and a radio that only sends back static,
but wakes to the sound of a helicopter the next morning.

　　　　I think the roar alone would stop my heart.
I walk into the woods by myself. Alaska rain. Evening.
It's the kind of forest someone dreamed up, moss a foot
thick, ferns and dwarf dogwood
on the floor—blooms that are perfect stars
to navigate back in time.
I may never return.
A hermit thrush calls its beautiful call,
like a meadowlark, but sadder.
Another thrush answers.
I look deep into the green
on all sides of me and watch,
talk to the bear.

The Bear's Heart

The bear's heart empties
onto the shore—small things

appear all at once
and some with urging:

a deer bone, a fistful
of dandelion, the curl

of a fish, a trumpet,
the words *not our darkness, spruce,*

sleep.

Whole mountains, a cave,
a steady rhythm.

*

Mother bear smells her cubs on the beach,
her head bowed low between her shoulders

teaching them the first lesson:
the promise

of red fish. Another mother
stares out a window. All glass is a river

slowly falling towards the center of the earth.
Gravity. A bright orange flower

on the other side of the pane.

She watches the hummingbirds drink—

Paradise Cove

A small yellow starfish spreads its six arms
against the palm of my daughter's hand.
Something that didn't fall from sky,
but was plucked from sea. She smiles for the camera.
The moon is playing tug-of-war with the earth
and for now the ocean gathers itself from shore—
children line up, holding the ends of a rope,
leaning all of their weight against each other.
When one of them lets go,
bodies tumble and the water hits the beach with surprise.
Right now I am looking out the window
of a cabin on a faraway shore with my parents.
We've waited our whole lives to see this view together—
a waterfall down the glacier, placid water reflecting blue sky.
Somewhere, underneath the glass
a whale's massive body glides.
Both years. The whales are there.
This year and the one before
the baby died. The one where I stood on the bank
in the dim dark and watched a bear in the grass
that turned out not to be a bear at all.
In the face of so much beauty,
something was looming past where I could see.
It took my breath away.
And now, I stand on the same shore,
full of grief and jump into the cold water
in the middle of the afternoon,
trying not to slip on the rocks,
no grace in my movement at all.
I can't find the bear.
She is with her cubs, far from our window
crisscrossing the river searching for fish.
We can't stop looking for her,
but she could care less.
This is the lesson. The starfish, the child,
the baby that was inside me dying, the baby inside me living,

the name, the song, the smell of low tide,
the rain filling up everything
the day we tried to leave town: no boats sailing, no planes.
Grounded. The wind hammered the shore.

The Bear's Mouth

1

When I look inside the mouth
when I reach inside
I can't find a hand
to pull her out.
I can't hold her on my lap
even as the bear stands
and sniffs the air between us.
All over the river there are bears.

2

The salmon are returning home. They fling themselves
out of the water at the falls
right on time to some song, some beat,
out and out and out, like popcorn
and a bear waits above the waterfall
all patience, all nonchalance. Opens her mouth wide
until they jump inside.

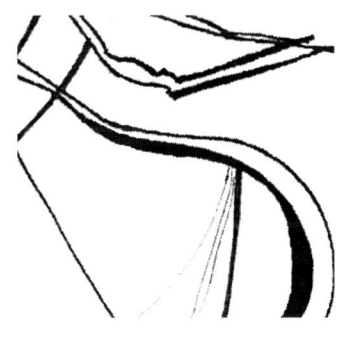

II

Before

If you pray hard enough, the miracle can happen. If you pray hard enough, you can save her life. We are only humans, we are not gods. Before the bear chose to save a lost boy. Before he kept him warm in the forest. Three years old. Before he didn't eat him, put his head inside his jaws. Before he kept the boy warm instead. I am not the angel my daughter sees out the window and calls a bird. *Mom, come see come see!* But we can still breathe in the sweet scent of alder and rain and we might save the bird from dying. Here, the world feels young. Like all of history hasn't touched the shore yet. Only the whale song, the ice song, the tree's slow whisper, the unwrapping of earth. Before war. Before religion. Before the glass broke. Before the land gathered together. Before we stood on the porch and watched the thunder and danced. Before they told me my second child would die. Before the king beheaded his wives. Before the ice melted. Before they found the mammoth in ice. Before the tiger crept through the grass and was gone. Before the frog song, before we stole corn. Before mom bottled peaches. Pears. Before she stroked my head while I cried. Before we taught our daughters to dance. Before a different bear in another time crept over my father's crib from an open window. Before grandma told me this story. Before the valley was filled with ghosts, before the light hit the valley, early, 3am, and a seal came up the river with the tide, before the rivers pumped blood into the body and before the body swelled, we are there together, watching it, the light and the rain on water. Something hits the surface. On the ultrasound screen she waves. A baby sleeps while the beast crosses over its crib into the room. His baby eyes open to bear. Inside, the beast hunts for something to eat. In your blood, that river. In that room you sleep in inside my body. Before the fish returned. Before the lost boy said the bear kept him safe. Before his mother wept and gathered him in her arms. Before the beast loved as much as it tears apart the fish, the deer, the bird. Before your heart stopped beating while I slept. We are not gods, not yet. Before I felt you slip out of my body onto a sheet. Before the whale rose to the surface and breathed air into the great lung of sky. Before I forgot to breathe. Before the sound of jets made me jump. Before the machine showed me your heart beat. Before more war. Before the children were taken from the room. Before their mothers knew what happened. Before the border closed. Before the orphans were lost. Before all the mothers wept. Before my father grew up and stepped out of that room with the bear behind him. Before we all looked the other way, the children on our screens. In a town, far from where we live now, where the shore of another country washes in. Next door. Before Jesus wept. Before the whale went from land to water. Before my daughters built castles on a beach. Before Mom pushed Dad in a wheelchair through the grove. Before he held the record for the 440-yard dash. Before I watched him catch fish after fish. Before the pilgrimage. Before he taught me how to fish. Before history slept in a book. Before history melted into a river. The river curls like a ribbon in the sunset and the fish feed like a dream. All of history in a hatch. Before her mouth shut a few moments after birth. All that's left, feathers on the beach. In a clearing, a few drops of red blood. Before the world began to spin. Before the water gathered together. There we were at the edge, ready, watching the river, sunlight catching our eyes.

Panorama

I am not Deinonychus, early Cretaceous,
scales or feathers on my elbows, ankles,
a fan of color around my eyes, claws that can tear out the jugular
in any neck free of armour. Oh, beating heart. Hunger.
Fountain of blood spilled on the mud.
And I am not Mammuthus Primigenius.
The smell of beastly body all earth and urine,
on a damp forest floor. A forest larger than any country or map.
Oh, to see what the sky was like back then. I am a woman
watching time from a hot air balloon rising.
I can see all the moments below me.
Each one getting smaller, crater from an asteroid,
the dust bowl rolling away, the towers' fall,
the houses I once knew, I can see them too,
tiny dots, faces gone to a blur of color
I can't distinguish. Voices rise as far as we may fly. 42 years. 500.
There, that lake is now a small jewel, fluid stone.
Water we dove into, *we* because it isn't always I,
eyes shut, nose plugged. Feel your body float
out of summer. Open your eyes and there is the wide mouth
of the bass, coming at you.

To the Brim

A well is beside my body
all the time, and the handle
that cranks up the bucket,
makes the sound
of a primeval animal
that's either extinct
or living behind my bedroom door.
Or this garden. This one next to the well.
Full of gourds, blossoms, and toads.
The water here is full of stars, a milky way
that spirals into the night
and if I pull it all up,
I can drink and be drunk
on what heaven is deep in the earth.
But what is lost there?
One hand carries the bucket.
Full of bones. Made of stars.
The girl who fell into the well
is never found.
My body turns into a branch of bougainvillea
growing wild. The one over the stairs
that lead down to the park
on the corner of Bonnie Brae and Bellevue.
Somewhere I used to live.
A galaxy of pink and red.

All of It

It has no name, this flower, this bird, this mountain we pray to,
the trail to the summit
where we'll hang a flag.
No name. The cats
will leave tracks, the ghost ones,
dogs too. Wolf or leopard. A friend, Tibetan,
takes us to a lake, iced over.
There we hang our flags on an auspicious day.
Burn the incense he takes out of a bag with his large hands.
He offers some to me and tells me what to call it.
But we don't speak the same language.
Kanchenjunga. Say it again.
I kneel because this is how I've been taught to pray.
I pray for the whole world. I do this again in another life.

In my backyard, twelve years later, a full moon,
winter solstice, we make a little fire.
I've kept the same plant he burned
and gave me
all this time.
When we hang the flags, I want to have more faith in the wind
to send the words to God, to the hearts of politicians,
to the hearts of human hands, to the ocean, to the center
of the earth. Here, this breath,
a bird that dives and dives and dives.

Deliverance

Last Christmas, your weight at birth
was one pound, thirteen ounces.
But there was so much water weight,
a tiny ocean under the skin,
the tide from my body to your body.
The moon your strong heart
that wouldn't stop beating.
I have a hard time calling it a birth,
you died on the way out. Your world
was my body. What do we call that day?
We'll pass it every year—
hang an ornament on the tree,
take the family into the snow,
feed the hungry. *Here is a plate*
of sweets.

I have a hard time reading the news.
Families walk the desert to cross a border
where troops wait.
The talk of walls, governments held hostage
by madmen. Children in cages.
Children dying in seizures
on one side of that line.
Already the news is tired
of telling us. But we are not helpless.
Hitching a ride to the border,
people cover the flat-bed
of a diesel truck. In the aerial view
they look like flowers in blossom,
summer, a float in a parade.
Will I greet them in my neighborhood,
thirty years from now? Or at a gate,
holding hands with their little one?
When and on what side
of the boundary will they die?

What is a birth
but crossing boundaries?
On the ultrasound screen you waved,
week after week and they swore
you didn't feel pain,
that you couldn't feel it
the same way I felt it.
The water seeped into your body
until you were crushed by the weight,
when everything inside you drowned.
0% chance of survival.
Until the day I woke up
and knew I had to deliver us both.
Little bird, in the end, I had to be the one
to kill you, to pull that plug.
I know there's a softer way to say it.
The night before, I floated in the bathtub.
We sang carols and Dad held his hands
on my belly—that line between us,
the space where you were.
Somewhere inside all of us
an imminent crossing,
the song and sound of ocean waves
crashing against the shore.

Colony Collapse Disorder

An entire colony of bees doesn't come back.
Every forager disappears while they are out looking
for the sweet. Thousands of them,
at the mouth of an orange poppy,
licking the fingertips of violet,
alfalfa, arrowleaf, drunk on summer.
All to survive what is to come.
But never finding their way home.
Where are all the lost? The women
who don't return from work. The women
who don't return with groceries.
The children taken at the border. The children
who run the bend on their bicycle
and are gone. Men who dig trenches,
tunnels underground. Whole families
into vans. A patrolman speaks to a screaming child,
but the baby doesn't speak anyone's language.
Someone goes for a hike and doesn't come back.
The mountain is trying to tell us where
to find them, but we don't understand.
Bees are at a mountain stream
drinking water that seeps
out of the earth. If you are slow
and quiet, make the right sounds,
the butterflies there will crawl
onto your finger. *This was the last time
anyone saw her.*

The Bear's Mouth

The earth just got smaller than the brains of the ants
living under the tomatillo in the crack of the patio.
This isn't their dream of sugar and sand.

In Los Angeles an alligator lizard soaks up sun
in the backyard of Sunset Blvd.
Banana trees thrive in this city that gets smaller
but has more people moving in.
The coastal temperate rainforests of Tasmania
and Alaska are shrinking. Spruce trees sigh, undeniably blue.
Next to a silver river, the lichen grows one millimeter per year
and the false azalea smells like skunk.
But it reminds you of your childhood.

All those summer nights when you opened a sliding door
to the stink of an animal somewhere in the dark.

The jaws of the bear unhinge.
On the beaches of France
the world is larger than it has ever been.
Orlando is carrying
five thousand times its weight
and those who march
are filling every banquet hall
with song. And sparrows
carry the mantra
straight into the heart.

Soon the entire world will fit inside
the brown bear's mouth.
Imagine stepping on the tongue.
The jaws are ready.

But in the belly of the bear
everyone is weeping and laughing
with every neighbor we don't have.

We've been walking for centuries
and crawled right in.

Prayer

The congregation is sitting in their pews,
heads bowed, like birds asleep,
except for one or two faces that are upright,
watching everyone else.
A brown bear has entered the chapel.
Her massive shoulders sway with each step.
She carries all the weight.
The man at the pulpit is still praying,
blessing everyone he has ever known
and everyone he doesn't and everyone
who is there and everyone who isn't.
The bear sniffs a purse. She grunts.
Bless the meek. Bless the blind.
Heads are still down and the bear
stands up on its back legs for a better view.
Bless the hungry.
The wild is what we came here for.
When she lands, it shakes the room.

In the Cemetery by My House Where I Take My Baby Girl Walking

We watch the cellophane windmills
next to the graves spin
and the autumn leaves spiral
into an unknown whirlwind,
some spirit catching them up, some devil.
This morning, a man and woman are frozen
in embrace. The sun has not yet risen.
They are both wearing black
and stand in front of the fountain,
next to the fake, bronze deer, perpetually
drinking. But as I get closer,
it's not a man and a woman.
It's only one man, and he's holding still,
leaning on a shovel. His oversized,
black sweatshirt makes two of him.
He's staring at his hands, holding
something small, like a metal worker,
peering over a piece of jewelry
two-hundred-years ago in a workroom
with a lamp burning. Except he's here,
standing in a field, surrounded by the dead.
The groundskeeper is beside him
in the muck of the fake pond, digging,
and suddenly my mother
is standing beside them both,
but they don't see her. She's holding
a garden trowel. What else existed
before there was time?
This is the coldest morning of winter so far.
And everything that isn't hiding
under something else,
is covered with the white face
of frost. Our breaths are small clouds,
small explosions in our skies.

Echo

The biologist holding the black bear cub does it casually. He looks like so many mothers I've seen in conversation, holding their babies, bouncing them while they talk. Swaying, patting their backs. He strokes the animal's fur and it claws at his jacket. He says the cub is eight pounds. The weight of my third daughter when she was born. The cub's mom is asleep behind him in a hollow log, still hibernating. I'm startled by the sight of her in her great sleep and imagine my girls poking their heads into such a space when we walk. The video switches to another bear that has denned under someone's deck. Two cubs born while she sleeps. I got here by typing "the heart of the bear", and the wording matters. In contrast, "The bear's heart" gives you all the pictures you'll ever need for a valentine: mostly, stuffed animals hold hearts like gifts in their paws. I also discover a group of scientists studying the heart of grizzly bears for the cure to heart disease. An echocardiogram hooked up while they hibernate. What are their hearts capable of that ours are not? The dangerous wild hooked to wires. But then I think, I am wild too. And here I am. We were once feral and sometimes we forget where our home is. Where we sleep. Just outside is that world. Where a mother bear is under your deck sleeping. It's only a matter of time. And there's a bear in the early morning dark, leaving her tracks in mud. Or she's sleeping next to my tent with her cubs, undiscovered, until we find the warm space in the grass. The shape of their bodies—one big, two small. Or she's behind me in some forest light, but I can't quite make out the shape. Or the bear is putting her nose in the air while we watch her over sunlit meadow and river. She's smelling something she can't quite see. She hears us all.

Baby Octopus Crawling on Hand

The octopus moves from behind
its rock in the DC zoo like a ghost,
a slow-motion illustration of how sound
moves in the inner ear.
The creature floats from one glass wall
to another, all eight arms
filling the space with octopus,
sucking us all in.
Once, we found one—a baby octopus
that I held in the palm of my hand
and watched and felt it press
as close as it could into my cold skin,
watched all eight arms change
to the pink color of my life-line
and callus. There it is. My life
disguised as octopus.
This is how to disappear.
Everyone gathers round
for nature's magic trick. Children press
closer, parents lean over, they're at the fair
and I'm holding a fortune-telling-scarab,
glowing with landscapes of their future.
None of us know as much
as we think we know.
I gently touch an arm
and the octopus changes
to a dark ocean brown,
quick and suddenly,
no longer a part of me,
back to being something
I shouldn't hold.

Waiting for Mammoths

On prime time,
they interview the scientist
who unearthed the great beast
and was up to her waist
in mammoth gore, up to her elbows
in frozen flesh. And you can see
the excitement as she describes
bile stones in the liver
and they show a picture
of what looks like two large beetles,
two large prehistoric brachiopods,
and for a second,
the camera is on the reporter
who looks as though
she is about to throw up.
But now, the scientist is telling us
about the blood that oozed out,
dark liquid, the thrill, the possibility
of complete DNA preserved
so perfectly in this mother.
Buttercup, they named the she-beast.
Didn't they promise
they would give us a mammoth?
I've been watching the headlines,
hillsides, roadside farms
for a glimpse. There is the question,
she says, *if we should?*
But you can tell she wants to.
How I long to see them
grazing on the islands,
their long wooly hair
blowing in the breeze,
their tusks making way,
filling the streets
with their saunter.
Deep in the bogs of time

if you passed them at sunset,
startled by their stillness,
you would take it as a sign.
In the mist, in Siberia,
I imagine saber-tooth tigers
and forests of ferns larger
than our houses, where we are nestled
and waiting for clones.
When we can't sleep, we'll arise
and step into the night
where we can almost see them
staring back, hear their nervous
breath. And we'll look up at stars
that may already be burned out.

Marbles Dropped By a Child's Hand Reflect Back like Eyes

Night in the garden, shining a flashlight.

Like creatures you see outside of camp or the roadside,
they're staring back at me from under the chives.

I reach down and pluck them from the face of the earth.
Each eye.

I carry them in my hand. Hear them clink in a bowl.
Imagine there are faces left behind, somewhere in the dark.

Rinse them under water.
Shiny orbs, a bowl of them.

One at a time, what visions they may lend us,
what futures we may behold.

III

Inside the Bear

Hold still. Listen
to the heartbeat.
If you close your eyes
and pay attention,
you can hear outside
            the dark room of bear
to the sound of the beast
walking on shore, searching
for something else to eat.
What did you think you would find in here?
Out there, the river has a mouth
that opens wide towards the ocean
where all the fish swim home.
In its depths, water breathes life
to everything that lives in the dark.
A silver flash. Purple stars
cling to rocks, a song moves, a sigh
in the tide slips further away—
where someone you love slides
into the beautiful sea.
Yet here you are. The bear sniffs salt,
you can hear the grunt.
She lifts her head. Inside,
curled in the black belly,
you watch the tunnel of throat,
waiting for what?

Hiding Place

I crawl into a space behind the rocks, under an overhang. There's too much noise. The sandstone is cold against my back. Everyone else is trying to nap. Cars pass by on the black snake road tracking the Colorado River. We made that snake, gave it a yellow stripe. The hissing noise of a hundred cars. An ant is silent on the sand searching for something sweet. In the breaks between noise a sob comes up in my throat. It never reaches air. The trees rattle. This holding back.

The nurses were playing some kind of game early in the morning while the mothers tried to sleep. They waged bets, and yelled and loud laughter clanged under every door. The mothers were waiting for their little ones. Some were afraid to fall asleep. Some knew their babies were going to die. Others were going to take them home dressed in little pajamas. Some were waiting to see the head crown and hear the cry. The nurses kept saying, *Try to sleep.*

The oak trees rustle. Sunlight filters through and creates halos on the earth. The ants continue their search. The nurses laugh louder. Someone wins the game. They cheer. Applause. The light from their desk comes under the door. Machines kick on. An ant crawls across my bare foot. A bird jumps up and down in the branches. Traffic follows a river that runs dry before it hits the border. Another country. A boundary I've never seen.

On the river, a raft carries the bodies of friends smiling in the sun. A raft carries bodies. The baby's heart won't stop beating. The midwife turns on the machine so we can listen to her live. Inside my body, she's floating. We know the baby won't survive the birth. *Do you want to record it? You won't have very much.*

The sandstone has been carved for centuries to create an arch. Some cliffs you can't see the top of. Some were painted by ancient hands. An ant is on my leg now. Under the clothing. I straighten my spine against the rock. A door slams shut. No one is sleeping. The machine breathes and counts my heartbeat. Blood pressure. Down the hall a baby cries. A father cries. A baby is slipping out. Silence. *Can you pick her up?* In this country, it's called a canyon. I stand up, my legs shake, the oak leaves are soft on one side. The baby is warm from the womb against my chest. The baby is cold. The baby's name means bird in another language.

A girl. Her skin weeps. The blanket is wet on our hands. The liquid from her body that wouldn't stop collecting water. On the screen you could see the water filling her up. All that black space in her lungs and around her heart. The stone against my back is red, orange, pink and black. A child laughs from a car window. An ant carries something large across the earth. The canyon is carved by the river, wind. The ant carries it home. How does she carry it? The hours tick. The swelling recedes from our baby's face. *There you are.* Her middle finger touches her thumb. What I remember most in grief. They are the tiniest hands I've ever seen. With the sweetest balloons on her skin.

Expecting

Mother bear can deliver her cubs
during her long winter sleep.
Less than one pound, and still,
the cubs know what to do.
They nurse and claw and climb
as their mother sleeps—the great beast.
The babies grow against her heat
while winter darkness slides
further away every day.
When I lie down at night
I have dreams that take me deep
into the mountains
where an animal waits in the dark space
under a tree. The smell fills my nose,
musk and wet earth.
Somewhere there is a cry
in the woods, a flash of wing
and your feet kick my rib
from the inside, then my liver.
You roll and yawn
in your dark space, both baby
and bear. An animal's heart
beats in the black
and my hands reach
to feel the rhythm
secreted in a cavern.
Outside the den,
the bear's claws
dig at decay—buried in the earth
is something she wants to eat.
Baby, when you come into the world,
how will it be?
Lights all over the room,
green medical gloves, gown open,
blood and vernix,
both of our heartbeats
tracked by a machine.

Claws That Can Reach the Heart

in one swipe, rip it out, are both mine
and yours. Look at your hands—
see how effortlessly you can do that?
The animal is a part of me
and a part of you. Her mouth
that lets out a rumble of water and thunder
is also my mouth and your mouth.
We have the same teeth and jaws.
And this beast can run faster
than a race horse. Even here, the length
from the river tinted with evening
to where we are standing, watching.
Ours is the 800-pound body
that keeps the one-pound bodies
of her cubs warm.
And they are all of our babies.
The bear eats her babies' scat
to keep them clean
in the dark nest of a winter den.
To know what it's like
to feel them climb and claw
our chest while we sleep,
while the winter sky falls down
above us and all around us, stars.
To eat enough for everyone.
The bear's mouth.
Hungry. Now, hear the heart
beating in front of you.
Life-giving drum,
something ancient and forever,
moving through water, forest, earth,
until it sounds its last in the song
it's been keeping time to so long.

Perseid Meteor Shower, 2020

We drive an hour into the mountains to get away from light to see other lights, pieces of a comet, littering our atmosphere with their flare. We are going to eat premade smores and lie on blankets and stare at the stars. The kids counted 14 deer on the drive up—nervous things on the side of the road. My daughter is holding a pink pony that is an inch and a half tall, clenched in her hand. Cousins are running all over, playing with flashlights now. I'm trying to get the one-year-old to sleep, but this life is too exciting, and she doesn't want to miss anything. Jane thinks she's lost her pony and the search party is on. A few minutes in, she's panicking. Months ago, she named the pony Heart. And now everyone is saying, *Where's Heart? Where's Heart?* With small beams of light we are searching the earth. It feels impossible to find. Until she realizes that there, the whole time, the pony was tight in her small hand. So used to it being there, she didn't realize she was holding it. What a good laugh we had. She sees the first shooting star in her life and ten minutes later is asleep under a blanket of them. Both of my girls on either side of me, I can hear their breath while I watch the sky. One beautiful flash after another. There and gone again. The last time I saw stars like this is lost in memory. *Look at that tail!* I used to be afraid a meteor would hit me one day. Leave a giant crater where I stand. On the drive home a mama deer and her two speckled fawns run in front of our car. We slow down and watch them. I've never seen baby deer so small. And they are gone into the forest as quickly as they appeared. What luck to get to see them. What life we have to live here. How we're so used to it in our hands.

Juneau, Alaska

A birthday party and a room full of musicians.
Through the window, we can see down to the sound
where the tide is going out, slowly slipping,
a giant mirror between mountains
where the western hemlocks weep clouds
into the blue of a midnight sun.

And here, here is a mandolin,
a violin, a bass, a banjo, a guitar,
the love of my life strumming.
The memory of what will be lost
somewhere in that future we cannot touch.

One woman with child,
one child shaking a leg in the air,
one father dancing across the room.
In the corner, holding a glass, someone cries
with happiness. Years ago, in the dim night of solstice,
this couple drove north up a highway,
chasing the sun.

Around every corner,
voices hang in the force of waterfalls.
Glaciers melting.
You would be surprised at how much water there is.
What shade of blue gets lost
then is recalled in memory?

And from all the strings,
the saddest song rises
like happiness in all of us.

Garden Before Isaac

After so many days of rain
weeds in the garden let go of the earth
with little coaxing.
I move with my body bent.
I want to bring the unborn baby closer
and closer to the earth
each day I go to it. This bed,
for sunflowers, this one,
tomatoes. Pulling one weed
after another. When Sarah
and Abraham were promised
a child in the desert, did she gather
sand just to feel the weight
of the grains in her fingers?
I clear the grass from the primrose.
I know that in a month's time
the blossoms will be open
and the primrose will take over
this bed of flowers. And I know
the hummingbird each time
it miraculously appears,
isn't trying to drink
my orange shirt,
but just can't seem to let
the color go. The earth is black
under my fingernails.
I still have not felt the baby move
and I'm afraid I never will.
Sunrise hits what night pearls
are left in the world,
before the sun changes everything
I think I know of living.

Dance

A bat circles above the crowd, looking for something to eat,
but all it finds is the sound of drums.
It chases every beat.

In my mother's garden, the flowers hold perfectly still,
offering orange and pink prayers.

This is summer.
Make room for the body.

Beneath

Think about the spirit of an animal that could occupy a house this big—the whale. There goes my first born, gliding past me at the pool with her dad in a man-made river, smiling and carrying the sun like she was born to do, making laps, there she goes again, wearing an octopus that floats. A mayfly lands on my arm, a messenger from another world filled with rivers, glass and ancient things. All the faces I've ever known are floating past now too—my third-grade teacher, my grandmother, the cashier at the market in L.A. Seagulls circle like vultures and bodies disappear into slides. There my daughter goes again, waving her hand as she rounds the bend. The surface of the pool is the color of tropics and chlorine. Footprints evaporate all around me. A toddler runs to the edge of everything and is scooped up just in time. Beneath all our feet, beneath arms waving, cheers and screams, the water opens wide, down there, a whale's massive tail disappears into the blue, its eye blinks, its body rolls. Sharks dance in the light, then disappear. There, a flash of iridescence. A fish. A silver school of them a mile long. A song yawns out of the deep.

What Chance I Had to See It

Driving freeway speed. Summer.
The air so hot you can see it wave,
a cellophane balloon, heart-shaped,
rises. String dangling below.
Free and dancing into the sky.
Some hand let it go.

The Heart of a Blue Whale Is the Size of a Small Car

A car I drive 70 miles an hour down a strip of concrete
with everyone I love the most inside.
My husband taps his knee with a pencil,
while one child is singing and the other is watching
her older sister intently. What will she do next?
Outside the blue whale's heart,
the girls see crows,
houses, a train. They name everything.
The lights of houses
as everyone looks past their own reflection
in the window
of the large heart.

A blue whale's heart beats 8-10 times a minute.
Between each beat you can tie your shoes.
Recite affirmations, hold still,
remember what it was you forgot,
choose your favorite song, before it beats again,
sing as loud as you want,
air drums, all of it,
with its two-mile radius of sound.

Inside the whale's artery,
an adult human can swim.
Imagine a heart that big—thousands of them
moving through the ocean, keeping
the largest animals that ever lived on earth alive.
Animals larger than TRex. Larger than the Loch Ness Monster.
It's the largest heart that has ever existed on earth.
And you could drive it home with everyone you love inside.

House of Dragons

I sing you the rainbow song
and the summer wind hits our faces.
You are one month old.
A cold front is moving in
and the trees shake their wild arms
like witches dancing.
Your older sister is asleep
dreaming something that will wake her.
Even when she's in my arms
I can tell her shouts are from another world.
She's not seeing this room or my eyes,
but *the house of dragons* she says,
I was trying to get out,
but I fell down.
Even as butterflies decorate the air above her.
And your other sister is with us,
here in the garden—
a gold finch or a white rose.
The trees shake like mad
in the breath of some serpentine creature,
something with wings.
The sky is a deep shade
of night. I hold you tight
against my chest, I'm scared
to set you down. To ask you your name.
Already you are too heavy
for my arms,
for this world.

Small Hearts

A moon rises and children parade
around the corner carrying
colorful birds in their hands.

They are so careful with their secrets.
They want to be asked, *What kind
of blue is your bird?*

This is childhood: In each doorway
they let one fly, exotic wings folding
still on the steps, behind
screen doors,

or disappearing, a small point
in a blank sky.
Birds flutter through hallways,

large white and iridescent
green feathers. They land on linoleum
kitchen floors, beside windows
that look on old back yards.

Door to door the children are gathering sweets
and a little boy dashes across the grass,
carrying something bright and orange,
its tail waving behind him like a flag.

One is given an apple,
another a bit of cake.
What kind of blue is your bird?

Stars

Marbles that burn at the touch
at the game you try to play

in the memory of childhood—
like grasping at the strings of a kite.

Cutting off the tail. Where did it go?
Burning balls of hydrogen helium

warm other planets
where there are blue craters,

eternal sunsets, and swirling mists of gas.
There are ferns growing under other suns

in the shade of rocks and dare
I say, houses. And above

is the blue canvas of twilight,
a quilt of sky sewn with the black

of hearts. Holes pricked
in that shade of night

so light can come through
the fabric, so it can dazzle

and wonder and cause you to gasp
when you stumble out of a tent,

somewhere deep in the woods,
far from where you are now.

Stars are made of memory.
Of glints from the eyes of animals,

of fear, cat's teeth,
fish bones, or scales

deep in the ocean. Of sand.
The hearts of horses, beating.

And they are up there, right now
keeping the beasts running across the sky.

And when you cut them open
after a death in a field,

after the great shudder, they are full
of light and exhaustion

and the smell of sagebrush after rain.

What Is Never Dead

Making music out of breath and hollow.
Where have I heard this before?
This vessel, this hollow sound.
My neighbor shoveling snow, the blade
against powder and concrete is like the sound
of someone blowing into a glass bottle.
All morning the snow has fallen,
small flakes to big flakes and back again to sunlight
or cloud. My neighbor leaves a pile of cat food
on the porch and every cat in the neighborhood has found it now.
Every day there is a new cat making music. It frightens me
because they sound the way we sounded
as babies crying. Someone out there is wanting.
He's also left piles of clothes, bikes, wires, glass pans, toys,
a sheep skull, a pile of sea shells, an old couch,
and the cats bed down in the grandeur of junk
and sleep next to the rats, pink eyes
like pearls, tunneling there too.
Winter's hand is in a fist this February,
but even still, underneath the cover
of ice and white, layer after layer, paw print
after paw print, the bulbs sleep and the grass sleeps
and inside the peach tree, the music of fruit
is waiting to sound its blossom cry.

Fear

Bear envy
is in my dreams.

I gather blueberries
and trail them behind me:

Come here little bear.

If you dare.

It is early morning and big claws
clamber

towards my sleep.

The Bear's Claw

You're downtown in an unnamed city. If you step out of your body
and look around, you can see it, the bear,

next to the creek that winds through a shopping mall,
trout swimming above the glitter of nickels and pennies.

Wishes from pockets and purses, gifts for gods.
There's the bear, fishing one out, a trout. He's ripping it apart

on the concrete. *World peace, a daughter
to come home, a cruise in the Caribbean,*

I wish she would say Yes.
Once, in the middle of the night,

the bear was on the lawn. Alaska.
I was up with a restless baby only calmed

by cold air. It was starting
to get light, but it was only 2am.

The kind of light only the north brings
and mist from the ocean. I sang that hymn,

a lullaby, and she fell asleep against my body,
my back to the house, my face to the bear,

trying to see it in the growing dream,
slowly taking shape in the dying night.

Which foot to put in front of the other,
which threshold to turn to, the door left open

behind me. The wild lapping
against the shore in front.

A child sleeping heavy against my heart.

Ode to All the Messy Rooms in My House

I praise you for your clutter of color,
the play dough creatures
mashed into the rug,
the small shoes sleeping under the couch.
For all the tiger marbles, the Sorry
board game cards littering my floors. *Sorry*
Sorry Sorry to the rose petals under the shelf,
to the beloved pony that has slept 600 nights
in my daughter's arms, now tucked
behind throw pillows waiting for rescue
from imagined hot lava on the floor.
Ode to summer's mint and lavender
hanging from the ceiling,
ode to the bag of treasures, leaves, grass,
collected all morning. Ode to winter's coats,
wet and dripping like the skins
of small animals shed at a warm door.
To the tired, old balloon—a pink cellophane star—
weeks past a birthday, resting here, bound to earth.
To the stockpile of art left by the five-year-old's hand,
this portfolio of smiles and snails and snakes,
of iguanas and trees, and sea anemones.
Treasure maps to her. To the bows
and puzzle pieces tossed by a toddler like confetti—
there's an eye of a fish
and a picture of Maine in one corner,
Arizona somewhere else.
To my couch dissembled—a fort?
Some place to hide in a jungle of here.
To the kitchen floor covered in
black beans running for the door,
noodles, mashed banana—whatever
didn't reach the baby's mouth.
Her fingers fat and learning, the awkward
reach of spoon, the proud smile.
The slobber of child kisses on a window.

To the jar of honey glowing on my ordinary table.
Time is neither here nor there.
O old sweet. O afternoon sunlight.
Gold of summer in the slant light of winter.
Ode to the peelings
of pomegranate and seeds, jewels everywhere.
O glove. O *wild and precious life*. O heart.

Living Forever

I don't want to die.
I want to stand forever at the edge
of this river, feet in the cold,
holding the hand of my daughter
where every so often, one of us reaches
into the water and pulls out a stone.

Look. Look at this one, we say.
From under the surface,
we find something smooth
and shining and pull it up.
This one has a stripe,
this one is the color of blood.
And then we carry it back to Dad on shore,
drop the prize into a heap.
Our new baby sleeps next to our pile of stones—

a rock cairn
for some traveler. A gold finch,
bright as a butterfly bounces
on the other shore.
What's between us?
I want her to live forever.

One week before, the baby was born.
I was startled by the heft of her body
against my chest. Her beautiful
smooshed face
and her cry. For a moment, that instant
before her breath, fear punched my heart,
I held my own, but then it came—

that cry I listen for down every moving hallway,
like a river. And there we were together, holding on.
Saying, *Look,*
look what I've found.

When You Crawl Outside of the Bear

you will always try to crawl back in.
Even when the world stops spinning
and a blue heron rises in front of you
like a dream you once had,
or the spirit of someone you love,
in the middle of a sunny afternoon at the water's edge.
A walk you're taking to see birds.
Something passing through on its way to another world.
Somewhere sunnier, probably.
In your hand a fly rod, something to draw
all the secrets out of the water. If only a bite, a strike.
There's always a bear, even when there isn't a bear.
And there it is, the fish caught on the bank, wriggling in the sunlight.
Sometimes the hook is out before you're even on your knees.
Hold the fish under water, feel it catch its breath
in your hands, before it disappears into some shadow place.
Somewhere you can't fit into. Not yet.

Notes

The artwork on the section breaks are fragments/details from a larger drawing done for this book by my mother, Susan Stott, from which we have made/are making broadsides.

"The Bear's Heart": *The first lesson* is a phrase taken from the title of a painting of a mother brown bear by Yukon artist, Nathalie Parenteau.

"Reaching Inside": *You have to be your own Cerberus* is something I once heard Robert Hass say in a Q&A session at Weber State University.

"In Sleep, Baby Jane" contains a line about the world beginning to spin. It's an image from a Marie Howe poem, "Part of Eve's Discussion," that has stuck with me for twenty-five years.

"Talking to the Bear" is a true story that happened to my friend, Dylan Morgan. Thanks, Dylan, for sharing it.

"Before" references a true story about my dad, told by my grandparents, about a bear walking across his crib, though it is debated among family whose crib the bear walked across. "Before" also references a true story about a boy in North Carolina: https://www.cnn.com/2019/01/28/us/casey-hathaway-bear-claims/index.html

"Claws That Can Reach the Heart": Here, I have to pay homage to Ada Limón.

"Ode to All the Messy Rooms in My House" ends with a line by Mary Oliver.

Acknowledgments

A thank you to the following journals and anthologies for publishing these poems:

All We Can Hold: poems of motherhood: "Garden Before Isaac"
Barrow Street: "Sisters"
Blossom as the Cliffrose: Mormon Legacies and the Beckoning Wild: "Stars"
Copper Nickel: "Monster"
Elysium Review: "Living Forever"
Kettle Blue Review: "Small Hearts"
Mid-American Review: "Colony Collapse Disorder"
River Heron Review: "The Dahlia Makes a Fire"
River Teeth, Beautiful Things Series: "Beneath"
Sugar House Review: "The Bear's Mouth"
Swwim: "Panorama"
Terrain.org: "When You Crawl Outside of the Bear"
The Rupture: "The Bear's Claw"
Wayfare: "All of It"
Western Humanities Review: "Baby Octopus Crawling on Hand" and
    "Waiting for Mammoths"

A huge thank you to Sunni Brown Wilkinson and Natalie Taylor. They offered me support, a space to cry, and valuable feedback on this manuscript time and again. Thank you to my dear friend Linda Cooper for her comments and wisdom, and Rob Carney for his feedback on an early version of this manuscript. Thank you to all of the Lynx House Press staff for their expertise and time. Thank you to Christopher Howell, for believing in and selecting this book, and like Jonathan Johnson and Nance Van Winkel, being a great mentor and friend (many thanks to them too). Thank you to my mom, for being my mother, a reader, and an artist for these poems, I appreciate her vision so much. Thank you to my dear dad, who held a copy of this manuscript before he died, and with mom, was always my biggest fan. Thank you to Katheryn Stott Buxton, my sister, for her beautiful painting for this cover. Thank you to Tim and Carol for being such a huge support to me all those summers in Alaska. Thank you to my midwife, Christy Francis, and the compassionate nighttime nurse,

Esmeralda. Thank you to all the poets and writers who have carved a way for more women's voices and the female experience in poetry. And most of all, thank you, dear Jake, for everything.